Tadpoles

Written and photographed by
Barrie Watts

Collins Educational

This young frog lives on land,

but frogs lay their eggs in water.

The eggs float to the surface of the pond.

They look like black dots covered in jelly.

The eggs start to change into tiny tadpoles.

The tadpoles swim out of the jelly.

They breathe through gills on the sides of their bodies.

The tadpole grows two back legs first.

Then it grows two front legs
and its tail begins to disappear.

The tadpole has changed into a tiny frog.

The young frog moves to the land to live.